Written by Jean-Pierre Verdet
Illustrated by Christian Broutin,
Henri Galeron and Pierre-Marie Valat

*Specialist adviser: Dr Anita McConnell,
The Science Museum, London*

*ISBN 1 85103 032 8
First published 1988 in the United Kingdom by
Moonlight Publishing Ltd,
36 Stratford Road, London W8*

The Moon and Stars Around Us

What do you see when the
Sun goes down?

At first the sky is still quite light, flushed pink where the Sun has set, then gradually it darkens to a clear blue-black. But look! There's a star shining brightly overhead. It's called the evening star, because it's the first to appear in the night sky. In fact, it isn't a star at all, though – it's Venus, a planet just like the planet Earth we live on.

Now the Moon is rising, and soon a whole host of stars can be seen glittering and twinkling in the sky. Try watching the sky night after night. There are all sorts of wonders to be seen...

Constellation of Taurus,
the Bull

Constellation of Leo,
the Lion

Constellations are the patterns that some stars make in the sky.

These patterns always reappear, and always look the same. For thousands of years, people have been giving names to the patterns. In the northern hemisphere most people know Orion, Pegasus and the Great Bear. Can you recognise them? (Check on p.31.) The best-known constellations are the ones which appear in the night sky all year long. They are the stars of the zodiac. Astrologers believe they shape our fates. But the stars are unconcerned with our little lives...

The Earth takes twelve months to pass the twelve constellations of the zodiac. Each constellation has a symbol and a name:

♊	Gemini	♒	Aquarius	♎	Libra
♉	Taurus	♑	Capricorn	♍	Virgo
♈	Aries	♐	Sagittarius	♌	Leo
♓	Pisces	♏	Scorpio	♋	Cancer

How can you recognise the Great Bear? And the Little Bear?

It is a big constellation made up of seven stars. Three of the stars are roughly in a line, the others shape a rectangle: it looks a bit like a saucepan. The two stars on the edge of the saucepan point towards the Pole Star, which is five times as far from them as the two stars are from each other. The Pole Star is the fixed point around which all the other stars in the sky seem to turn. It marks the north, and is at the edge of the handle of another, smaller saucepan shape: the Little Bear.

Little Bear

Great Bear

The Great Bear and the Little Bear revolve every night around the Pole Star, moving like the hands of a clock, only backwards. Even during the day, when you can't see them, the stars go on moving and making their patterns.

11

The Earth spins round
as it circles the Sun.

How does
the Earth move?

If the stars seem to
revolve around the Pole Star,
if the Sun rises every morning and
sets each night, it's all because the
Earth is spinning round, like a
spinning-top. The axis of the Earth's
spin meets the sky close to the Pole
Star, which is why the star doesn't
seem to move. But the Earth doesn't
just revolve on itself, and give us day
and night, it also circles round the Sun
– that trip takes a year. So, though the
ground seems solid and still to you, in
fact our planet is spinning round and
hurtling through space. The first
person to discover this was an
astronomer called Copernicus, over
four hundred years ago.

◄ Our planet, the Earth

13

A giant step: walking on the Moon

Throughout the ages people have always been fascinated by the Moon. Some have seen a face in the patterns on its surface, others a person or an animal. If you promise somebody the Moon, you are promising something impossible, and it always seemed impossible that men should actually walk on the Moon, until one day in 1969, when the American Neil Armstrong stepped out of his spaceship on to that dry and dusty surface.

If there were no Sun, we wouldn't see the Moon.

The Moon is cold, and does not shine. The moonlight we see is actually sunlight reflected back from the Moon. When you look at a full Moon in the sky, you can see dark patches on it. They are called **seas**, even though there isn't any water on the Moon. They are huge plains covered in grey dust. The **mountains**, which look like bright spots, are very high and irregular. If you look at the Moon through a good pair of binoculars, you'll be able to see the different kinds of surface: the Moon is covered with craters and ditches of all shapes and sizes.

The Moon is smaller than the Earth. It has a diameter about a quarter the length of the Earth's.

The phases of the Moon

The Moon revolves round the Earth. Even so, if the Moon shone with its own light, we would always be able to see it, and it would always seem full. As it is, though, the Moon and the Earth are both lit by light from the Sun. This means that how much of the Moon we see depends on its position in relation to the Earth and the Sun. Sometimes we can see the whole of the Moon, sometimes only part. And occasionally, when it's in a position between us and the Sun, we can't see it at all.

These regular changes are called the phases of the Moon.

If we lived on the Moon, we would see phases of the Earth. These are what some of them would look like.

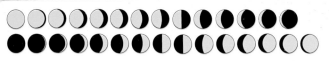

These are all the phases the Moon goes through in 27.3 days, which is a lunar month. A lunar month is just a little bit shorter than a calendar month.

You can see here the different ways in which the Moon moves with the Earth. The diagram below shows why the Moon appears to us to move through its phases. As the Earth (1) rotates on its axis, the Moon (2), with one of its hemispheres lit up by the Sun, moves in orbit round the Earth. Each night we see different amounts of the part which is illuminated (3).

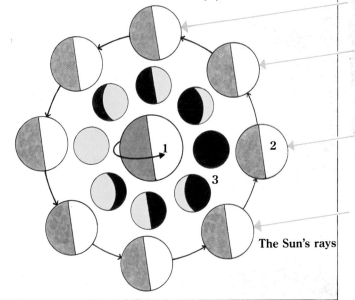

The Sun's rays

The Moon is on the opposite side of the Earth to the Sun. It is fully lit. It is highest in the sky at midnight; this is a full Moon.

Four days later, the Moon doesn't reach its highest position in the sky until three in the morning. You can't quite see it all.

Four days later, the Moon is in its last quarter. It is two o'clock in the morning. The moon only rose an hour ago.

It is eight in the morning. The Moon is getting thinner – it is waning. As it climbs the sky, the daylight makes it invisible.

There's a new Moon, but you can't see it because it is between us and the Sun.

Five days later: the Moon has moved away from the Sun, and you can see it again. It is seven in the evening. It will soon set.

The Moon moves into the Earth's shadow. It gets darker and darker, then for a little while it disappears altogether.

Lunar eclipses

Month after month, the Earth and the Moon play hide-and-seek with each other. And because the Earth stands in the sun's light, it throws a shadow, just like you do. So sometimes in this age-long hide-and-seek, the Moon finds itself passing through the Earth's shadow. It looks as if it's gradually being nibbled away. In times past, people thought it was being eaten by a dragon!

But don't worry, the Moon always reappears – it's only an eclipse. There is usually about one lunar eclipse a year.

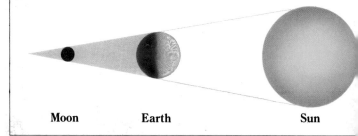

Moon   **Earth**   **Sun**

The Earth doesn't travel round the Sun on its own. As well as the Moon, it has eight other travelling companions: **the planets of the solar system.** Some are small, like the Earth, and with a solid, rocky surface. These are Mercury, Venus, Mars and Pluto. The others are huge and surrounded by gas: Jupiter, Saturn with its rings, Uranus and Neptune.

Nearest the Sun is Mercury; then come Venus, the Earth, Mars, Jupiter, Saturn, Uranus, Neptune and Pluto. The picture shows the planets' sizes in relation to each other, but not the distances between them – to do that, this book would have to be over a kilometre wide!

But all the planets, like the Earth and the Moon, are cold, and only reflect light from the Sun.
As well as these eight, there are a whole lot of tiny planets, crowded into the sky between Mars and Jupiter. They may perhaps be part of a planet which has broken apart.

Pennies from heaven

Not everything in space moves with the ordered harmony of the stars and planets. Comets and meteors come and go.

In 1908 a meteorite fell into a forest in Siberia. Meteorites as big as this are very rare.

Comets are small, intensely bright balls with a wide tail of gases. They travel from the far reaches of the solar system, come close to the Earth and then go away again. Meteors are the rocks of the solar system. When one of them passes close to the Earth, it is captured by the Earth's gravity and falls, burning up in the atmosphere. This is called a 'shooting star'. Sometimes, meteors are too big to burn up, and fall to the ground as meteorites.

This Crater in Arizona was created by a falling meteorite over 100,000 years ago.

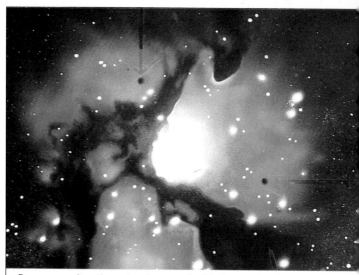

Stars are often born in clusters inside huge clouds of hydrogen. Throughout the universe there are stars being born all the time. Using a very powerful telescope, it is possible to see stars being formed in the Triffid nebula.

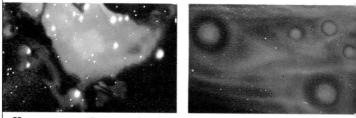

How stars are born: a cloud of gas and dust begins to contract. It will give rise to one or several stars.

The more the cloud contracts, the hotter the gases inside become. When they are hot enough, the star begins to shine.

How do stars live and die?

Stars are huge balls of very hot gases.
The hotter stars are, the whiter their light.
The burning gases give off heat and
light as their main gas, hydrogen, is
transformed into another gas, helium.
This transformation gives off heat
over billions of years.

But **in the end, stars go out**: they
explode, if they are too big, or they cool
down if they are too small. **Our
Sun is a star**. It is a medium-
sized star, neither very big, nor very
small. It is several million degrees
centigrade at its centre. It has been
burning for about 5,000,000,000 years.
It is about halfway through its life.
In another 5,000,000,000 years or so,
it will get cold and go dark.

When all its hydrogen has burned away, a star may swell up: it
is a red giant. Then it explodes inwards: it is a white dwarf.

Looking south in winter in the northern hemisphere

Looking south in summer in the northern hemisphere

Star-gazing

If you want to watch the stars, choose a clear, cloudless night when there isn't a Moon: the Moon's brightness makes it harder to see the stars. You can watch the stars through binoculars or a telescope, but even with the naked eye you can see more than two thousand five hundred stars!

If you look at the sky in winter, facing south, these are some of the constellations you can try and find:

1. Orion
2. The Bull
3. The Pleiades
4. Perseus
5. The Ram
6. The Charioteer
7. Andromeda
8. Pegasus
9. The Fishes
10. Aquarius
11. The Whale
12. Eridanus

And in summer, if you face in the same direction, you might see these:

1. The Lyre
2. Hercules
3. Ophiucus
4. The Crown
5. The Wagoner
6. The Virgin
7. The Scales
8. The Archer
9. The Goat
10. Aquarius
11. The Fishes
12. Pegasus
13. The Dolphin
14. Altair
15. The Swan
16. The Serpent
17. The Scorpion

This is an observatory. It has a powerful telescope for seeing very small and distant stars.

This is our galaxy, the Milky Way, seen from the side. The little arrow shows the position of our Sun and of the Earth.

Our Sun, our star, is not cut off from the universe. It is one of a huge, flat cluster of millions of stars which we call **the galaxy**. The galaxy revolves around itself in a long, slow movement lasting 250 million years. Yet another movement we're not conscious of here on Earth! The universe is filled with millions and millions of galaxies like ours, forming different groups and patterns just like the stars and planets.

Between the galaxies there are the nebulas – great clouds of gases and dust. They shine brightly as a star is born: that is what is happening in the Triffid nebula at the moment.

◄ If we could travel beyond our galaxy and look down on it from above, it would look like this.

Ptolemy, astronomer
Greece, second century AD

Copernicus, mathematician
Poland, 1473-1543

Kepler, astronomer
Germany, 1571-1630

Galileo, astronomer
Italy, 1564-1642

Newton, mathematician
England, 1642-1727

Einstein, physicist
Germany, USA, 1879-1955

"If I have seen far, it was because I was standing on the shoulders of giants." That is what the great English mathematician Isaac Newton said. These are some of the giants he meant, and one, perhaps the greatest of all, who came after him.

Ptolemy lived in Alexandria. He believed that the Earth stood still at the centre of the world. His book on astronomy, the *Almagest*, was the most important book on the stars for nearly 1,400 years.

Nicholas Copernicus made calculations which overturned Ptolemy's astronomy. He showed that the Earth revolved every 24 hours, and went round the Sun every year. The Earth was an ordinary planet like any other.

Kepler discovered that the planets don't move in circles but in ellipses. He worked out the laws of these elliptical orbits.

Galileo was the first astronomer to use a telescope to study the sky. That was in 1609. He saw all sorts of new marvels: the satellites of Jupiter, the rings of Saturn and the mountains of the Moon.

Newton was a mathematician, physicist, chemist and astronomer. He worked out the laws of gravity. Gravity keeps the Earth in its orbit and us on the Earth.

Einstein was the most outstanding thinker of the twentieth century. Born in Germany, he lived most of his life in America. He worked out the Theory of Relativity, and changed our view of the universe, from the infinitely big to the infinitely small, and of time itself.

Index